Rainforests

PEOPLE
& PLACES
IN PERIL

General Editor :
Alexander Goldsmith

Rainforests

BY SARA OLDFIELD

Photographs by Still Pictures

CHERRYTREE BOOKS

Photographs supplied by
Still Pictures

A Cherrytree Book

Edited and produced by
Philip Clark Ltd
53 Calton Avenue
London SE21 7DF

Designed and typeset by
Hans Verkroost

Maps by
European Map Graphics Ltd

Artwork by
Mike Atkinson

First published 1995
by Cherrytree Press Ltd
a subsidiary of
The Chivers Company Ltd
Windsor Bridge Road, Bath
Avon BA2 3AX

British Library Cataloguing in Publication Data
Oldfield, Sara
Rainforests. — (People & Places in Peril Series)
I. Title II. Series
304.209152

ISBN 0-7451-5218-X

Printed and bound in Italy by L.E.G.O. s.p.a., Vicenza

CONTENTS

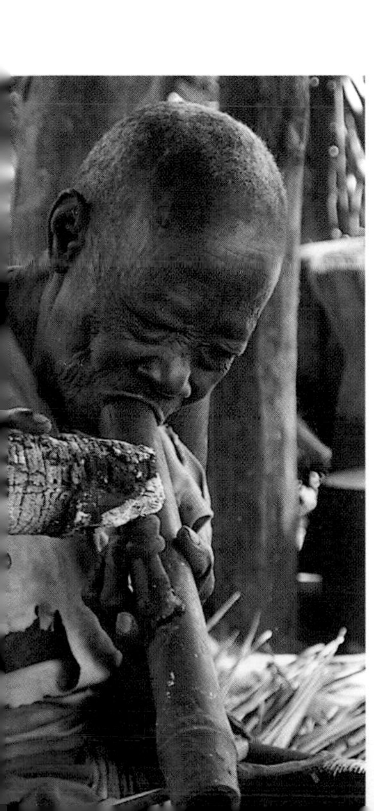

UNDERSTANDING RAINFORESTS

It is difficult to imagine a rainforest if you have never been in one. The trees are very tall and densely packed together. Their leaves form a thick ceiling that the light hardly penetrates. At ground level, undergrowth can make it difficult to move about. Some people have called the rainforest a 'green hell'.

But to the people who live there, the rainforest is a friendly place. There is always plenty to do — hunting or fishing — and plenty to eat. The forest is home. It is also school, farm, playground and church, all rolled into one.

Living in the rainforest is not easy. You can starve to death if you do not know how to find food. But the local inhabitants, the indigenous people, have developed all kinds of ways of making the best of the forest. And since they know that the forest provides all life's essentials, they have always treated it with respect.

Over the last 500 years, as people from western countries have explored and colonized the world, they have introduced changes. In their search for new resources — gold, timber, rubber and land — they brought the modern world to the rainforest. In doing so, they have put rainforests and the people who inhabit them in peril.

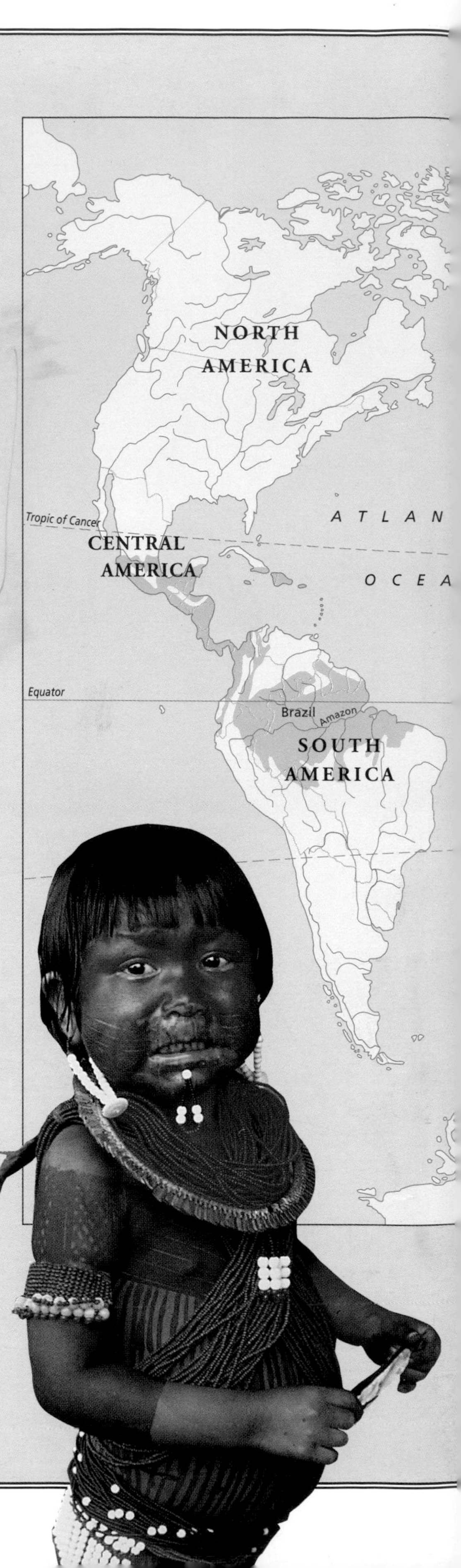

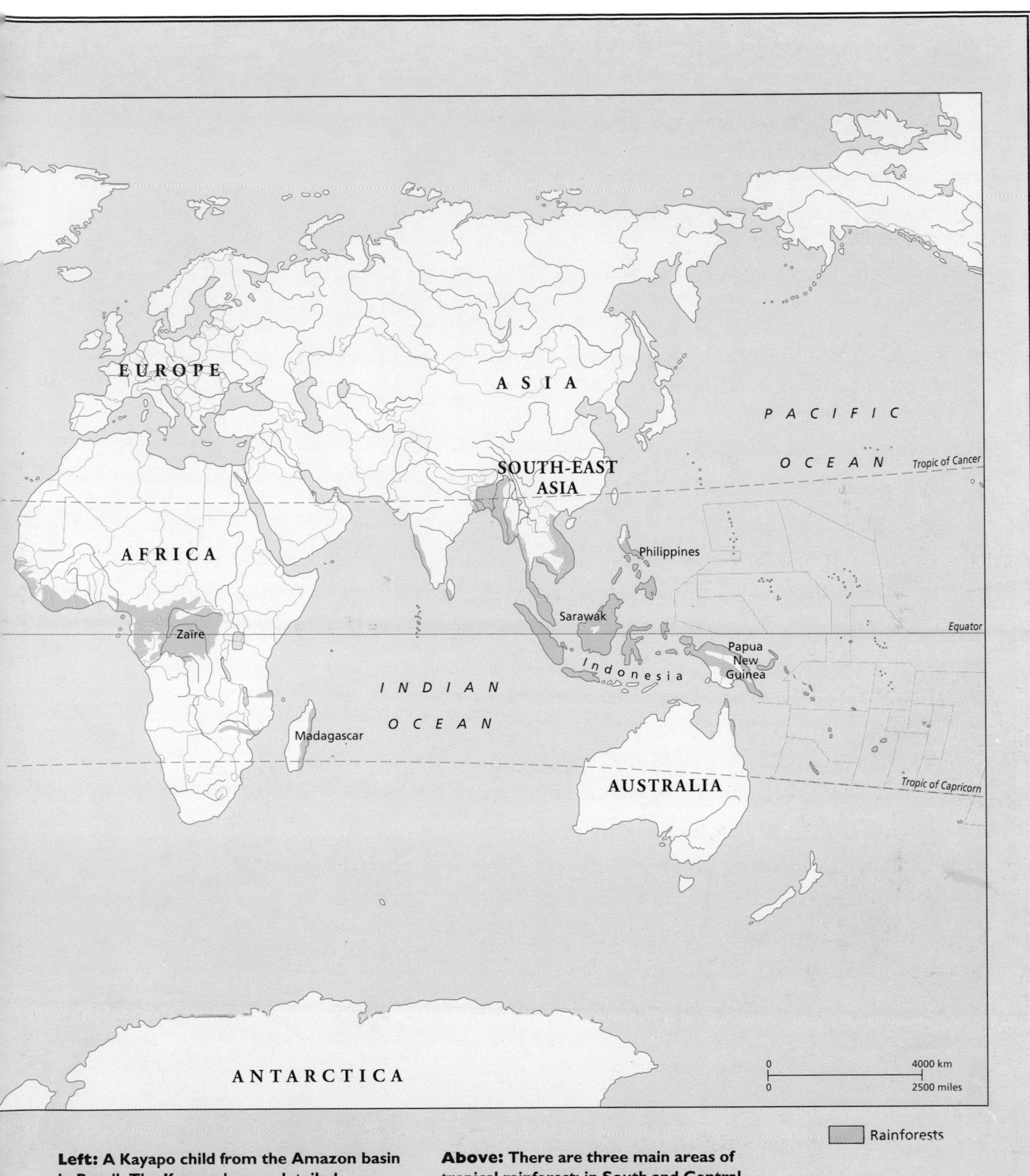

Left: A Kayapo child from the Amazon basin in Brazil. The Kayapo have a detailed knowledge of rainforest plants and animals. They live by hunting, farming and gathering forest fruits. They decorate their faces using red dye from a plant called urucum.

Above: There are three main areas of tropical rainforest: in South and Central America; in Central and West Africa; and in South-east Asia, particularly the islands such as Papua New Guinea that lie between the mainland of Asia and Australia.

The Structure of Rainforests

The tropics are that part of the Earth bounded by the tropic of Cancer to the north of the equator and the tropic of Capricorn to the south. Here, the climate is hot all year round. The tropics receive more sun than areas further to the north and south. There is no winter or summer, just a rainy season and a dry season.

Large parts of the tropics are covered with forest. Where there is a lot of rainfall it is known as rainforest. Tropical rainforests are among the richest habitats in the world. The lush rainforests of Africa, Central and South America, and parts of Asia taken all together cover only six per cent of the Earth's surface — yet they contain about half the world's species of animals and plants. The world's biggest rainforest, in the Amazon, covers six million square kilometres (2.3 million square miles), an area over half the size of Europe.

There are several layers in a tropical rainforest, and each layer has its own animal inhabitants. The tallest trees are called emergents. Below them comes the dense canopy of tree crowns. The understorey consists of smaller trees, shrubs and ferns. The lowest layer is the forest floor.

The Canopy

Rainforest trees seem to crowd each other to reach the sunlight. Their crowns form a thick, leafy layer, known as the canopy.

The canopy is usually 30-40m (100-130ft) above the ground. Some giant trees, known as emergents, soar high above the canopy. Beneath the green umbrella of the canopy is another layer of trees, the understorey. This is about 15m (50ft) above the forest floor. There are many palm trees at this level.

Life high in the rainforest canopy has until recently remained a mystery. Trees reaching the height of an eight-storey building are extremely difficult to climb. So scientists who want to study the forest roof need to build special towers and aerial walkways. Research is now showing the extraordinary richness of life in the rainforest canopy.

The tree crowns support a wide variety of plants which use the tree branches for support. Orchids, bromeliads and ferns are some of the plants which grow high up in the forest. These in turn provide homes for countless species of insects.

Right: The tall trees of tropical rainforests are difficult and dangerous to climb. Even the forest inhabitants sometimes fall to their deaths climbing trees to collect honey, for example. Researchers who wish to study the canopy of a tropical rainforest often build aerial walkways, like this one in Malaysia. The canopy is the home of most rainforest animals, such as birds and monkeys. Trees compete with each other to reach the sunlight.

Bird life is also abundant in the upper layers of the forest. Treefrogs, flying lizards, bats, squirrels and monkeys are at home in the treetops. There are more animals in the canopy than anywhere else in the forest.

The Forest Floor

The forest floor is a dark and mysterious place where little light penetrates. Hot, damp conditions and plenty of fungi and bacteria make sure that leaves and other plant material falling to the ground will quickly rot.

Relatively few shrubs or flowers grow at ground level in the forest. Many of the seeds of the forest plants lie dormant in the soil until a large tree crashes to the ground. The resulting gap in the forest canopy allows light to penetrate to the forest floor. Then the seeds can put down roots and grow up towards the sun.

The luxuriant growth of rainforests depends on the rapid recycling of the nutrients. The soils underneath the forest cover are often poor in quality. This is because the goodness in the soil is quickly taken up by growing plants. That is the reason why, once the plants are removed when the rainforest is cleared, the thin, infertile soils rapidly break down and get washed away by the heavy tropical rainfall.

Primary and Secondary Forests

Undisturbed areas of forest are known as virgin, or primary, forests. Secondary forests are those that grow in areas that have been cleared. They usually have fewer species, often with faster-growing trees. There are fewer forest layers, and the forest floor is more tangled than in the primary forest. More shrubs, lianas (climbing plants) and young trees are able to grow because there is more light.

Left: The tallest trees of the Amazon rainforest reach up to 60m (200ft) above the ground. Many different kinds of tree are found within the forest. In one single hectare (2.5 acre) plot of Peruvian rainforest, 300 tree species have been identified. Compare this with 700 tree species in the whole of North America.

VARIETY OF LIFE

The variety of life in an area — the number of different species — is known as its biodiversity. As we have already seen, tropical rainforests cover only about six per cent of the Earth's surface, but they are home to over half the world's species. This means that rainforests are very rich in biodiversity. Eighty per cent of all known insects are found in tropical forests.

South and Central American forests are thought to have the greatest biodiversity, followed by the forests of South-east Asia. It has been estimated that the rainforests of the Amazon have over one million plant and animal species.

No one knows for sure why tropical rainforests are so rich in biodiversity. One possible reason is that these forests have evolved in the same place over millions of years, allowing many different life forms to evolve. The hot, wet climate and soil conditions also provide part of the explanation. High energy input from the sun and heavy rainfall encourage luxuriant plant growth.

Most of the world's parrots live in tropical forests. Many, such as this hyacinth macaw, the largest species of parrot, are threatened by habitat destruction and collection for the pet trade. Now there are only about 2500 hyacinth macaws left in the wild. About 100 parrot species, roughly one in three of the world's total, are at risk of extinction.

Below: Rainforests are rich in colourful plants, such as this Heliconia. This fact helps to explain why Ecuador, a relatively small country, contains more different plant species living in the wild than the whole of North America.

Right: Tree ferns commonly grow in rainforest areas. Some species do very well in secondary forests but others have become very rare as the primary forest is destroyed. In some countries tree fern trunks are used to make carvings believed to have magical powers. Elsewhere tree ferns are chopped down to make special potting compost for orchids.

'Hot Spots'

Biodiversity is not evenly spread throughout the tropical rainforests. Some areas, especially rich in biodiversity, are known as hot spots. These areas are also suffering from rapid forest loss. Ten tropical forest 'hot spots' cover less than one per cent of the Earth's surface, and make up 3.5 per cent of the primary forest cover. These small areas contain over one quarter of all tropical forest plant species.

One of the forest hot spots is an area of Colombia in South America. The rainforests of the Choco region have not been fully explored but are already known to be richer in plants than anywhere else in the world. The Choco is also very rich in birds. It has over 100 different bird species found nowhere else.

The white uakari is found only in the rainforests of the Upper Amazon. These monkeys, with their extraordinary red faces, live in troops of 50 or more. Uakaris are rare because so many have been hunted for food. Now the white uakari is protected by law.

Interdependence

Many of the different plants, animals and people within the rainforest depend on each other for survival. Insects and birds are needed to pollinate the flowers of rainforest trees. The fruits provide food for a wide range of animals and humans. This is all part of the rich pattern of rainforest biodiversity. Left to itself, the rainforest is a stable ecosystem. However, when pieces of the biodiversity jigsaw are removed, no one knows what the long-term effects will be.

Rainforest Research

No one knows how many different species there are on Earth. Recent estimates range from five million to 30 million. In any case, only about 1.4 million have been described and catalogued by scientists. New species are being discovered almost every day in the tropical rainforests. Most of these are insects and plants such as mosses, fungi and algae. But new discoveries of monkeys and birds are still being made. Several new monkey species, for example, have been found in the Atlantic coastal forests of Brazil in recent years.

Some species are so localized that destroying a few hectares of rainforest can render them extinct. The significance of such a loss is difficult to calculate. Many plant species have been of enormous value to us, both commercially and in terms of our standard of living. Many rainforest plants have been found to be biologically active against a range of serious human diseases.

Rainforest Research

Unfortunately, not enough scientists have been trained to identify tropical species. Most of the experts live outside the tropics and work in universities and research centres in the United States and Europe. They plan expeditions to the areas where more survey work is needed. Computers are making it easier to store information on the thousands of species found in the rainforests and to exchange information with experts around the world.

Much of this research depends on the extensive knowledge that indigenous people have about their environment. In the past, they were quite happy to share that knowledge with western scientists. More recently, they have realized that their valuable knowledge represents a bargaining counter. They can use it to negotiate fairer and better protection for themselves and for their forest. Nowadays, western scientists are expected to work with local people and share the results of their work with them.

Above: Cataloguing and recording leaf types and sizes as part of a project involving studying forests in Kenya, East Africa. The use of computers has made the job of storing information on thousands of plant species much easier.

A Poison that Cures

Many surgical operations today are aided by a drug that was originally used by Amazonian Indians as an arrow

poison for hunting. Known as curare, it was first noted by European explorers in the 16th century. But for some 200 years, no one knew where the poison came from or how it killed its victims.

Only in the 19th century did scientists begin to unravel the mysteries of curare. They discovered that the poison worked by blocking the messages sent by the brain to control muscles in the body. Without these impulses, the muscles become flabby and the victim dies of suffocation.

Some time later, scientists also discovered that if they helped the victim to breathe artificially, sooner or later, he or she would recover fully. Today, curare, or one of its artificial substitutes, is used in sensitive operations where the patient's muscles have to be relaxed. It is also used in the treatment of Parkinson's disease.

Above: The dense green rainforest canopy may be up to 6m (20ft) thick. In tropical rainforests, many of the trees are evergreen and do not lose their leaves as many trees of northern countries do in the winter. Different trees flower at different times throughout the year. Vines and lianas scramble up the tall trees to reach the sunlight in the canopy.

Inset: Biologists in Ecuador are recording the species they find in the rainforest. Ecuador's lowland rainforests, to the east of the Andes mountains, are some of the richest and most threatened forests in the world. Biologists set up a temporary research station, living and working in tents. They take specimens of plants and insects to identify, some of which may be new to science.

Controlling the Climate

Around 25 per cent of all the people in the world depend on the water from tropical forests. The trees and soil of the forests act as a sponge storing much of the rainfall from tropical downpours. They stop water running straight off the land into rivers and the sea.

Rainforests are the most important water store because they grow in the wettest parts of the tropics. When the forests are cut down, the result may be water shortages in nearby areas. Further away, heavy tropical storms can produce devastating floods when there are no forests to soak up the water.

The Mirror Effect

Rainforests also absorb heat from the sun because they form a dark surface. They are like giant air conditioners, working on a global scale. When the trees are chopped down or burnt, the crops or grass that replace them are much lighter in colour. Instead of absorbing heat, they reflect more of the sun's heat back into the atmosphere. This is known as the mirror effect. The changes in temperature affect air circulation in the atmosphere. This can alter weather patterns thousands of kilometres away.

The Greenhouse Effect

The tropical rainforests act as a store of carbon dioxide. This gas is present in the atmosphere, and is used by plants to make food. When rainforest is cut down and burnt, large amounts of carbon dioxide are quickly released back into the atmosphere.

Carbon dioxide is a greenhouse gas. It traps the sun's heat in much the same way as a garden greenhouse. So increasing amounts of carbon dioxide in the atmosphere are causing global warming. Many scientists believe that tropical deforestation contributes about 30 per cent of the build-up of carbon dioxide. Burning oil and coal adds much of the rest. Car fumes in Europe and the United States are also one of the main causes of global warming. Some scientists have predicted that global temperatures could increase by as much as 3°C (5.5°F) by the end of the 21st century.

Above: The Maldive Islands in the Indian Ocean are exceptionally low-lying — rarely rising to more than about two metres (6ft 6in) above sea level. Some scientists believe that sea levels may rise by some 20cm (8in) by the year 2030 through the melting of polar ice as a result of global warming. Rises in the sea level on this scale would mean that parts of the Maldives and other low-lying countries would be under water.

The Mirror Effect

Above: Dark colours absorb heat from the sun, while light colours reflect it back. The dark green of the rainforest canopy absorbs the sun's heat. When the rainforest cover is removed, it is likely to be replaced by vegetation that is much lighter in colour. This reflects back the sun's heat into the atmosphere, instead of absorbing it — the Mirror Effect. Such changes can affect weather patterns over considerable distances.

The Greenhouse Effect

Left: By trapping the sun's rays and absorbing their heat, atmospheric gases such as carbon dioxide help to keep the Earth warm. Without this 'greenhouse effect', life could not survive. Recently however, deforestation, fossil fuel use and other activities have added to the concentrations of carbon dioxide and other gases. Scientists believe that this 'global warming' could have far-reaching climatic consequences.

RAINFOREST PEOPLE

Some people imagine that the rainforests are uninhabited, still waiting to be visited by intrepid explorers. In fact, tropical rainforests have been occupied for thousands of years and even today are home to about 140 million people.

Some of these people are the original indigenous inhabitants who have lived in the same place for generations. Such people traditionally lived in harmony with the plants and animals. They took from the forest only what they needed in order to live.

Traditional Knowledge

Over the centuries, indigenous people built up a great store of knowledge about the precious resources of the rainforest. The Hanunoo people of the Philippines, for example, can distinguish between 1600 different plants in their forest, 400 more than scientists working in the same area.

Such knowledge is combined with a strong feeling of respect for the rainforest — so strong, in fact, that strict rules help to protect it. Rainforest peoples have also been excellent guardians of their environment — so good, that it is often difficult to tell that they once occupied a particular area.

Left: An Ndorobo forest dweller from Kenya, East Africa, collects honey from one of his many hives. Climbing the tall trees of the rainforest in search of this highly-prized food is dangerous, and a fall can be fatal. Occasionally, a large tree is cut down so that honey can be collected from beehives high in its branches.

Below: Yanomami Indians from the Orinoco River basin in Venezuela. The Yanomami are South America's largest rainforest tribe. They were first contacted by people from the outside world as recently as 1950. They obtain their food by combining hunting and gathering with shifting cultivation.

Living in the Rainforest

Rainforests are such rich and diverse places that they offer many different opportunities for humans to make a living. The simplest and oldest way is hunting and gathering. Here, people merely live off the natural bounty of the forest. They hunt wild animals for meat and collect wild plants and fruits for their vegetables. They also use the forest as a source of medicines and tools. Hunting and gathering has less impact on the rainforest than any other human use.

Rainforest communities are small. The supply of food is not sufficient to support large permanent settlements. As a result, hunter-gatherers do not take more from the forest than it can naturally regenerate.

Customs and Beliefs

Often, there are special customs to make sure that useful plant and animal species survive. For instance, the Tukano Indians of Brazil believe that certain sections of their river are the resting places of their

Above: Slash and burn agriculture near the Rio Branco in Amazonia. Burning the forest is the quickest way of clearing it to grow crops. However, the land will soon lose its fertility, and the farmer will be forced to clear yet more forest.

Left: A migrant farmer in Peru clearing land for cultivation. The relentless demand for land is one result of increasing population growth. New settlers are desperate to grow crops to feed their families. But cutting into the rainforest from the outside (as opposed to clearing small patches within it) prevents it from regenerating.

ancestors and should not be disturbed. As the Tukano well realize, this also helps to preserve and restock the fish population on which they depend for their protein.

Such beliefs and customs, passed on from generation to generation, are part of the knowledge that makes survival possible in the rainforest.

Small groups of hunter-gatherers still live in all three rainforest regions. Altogether, about one million people live by hunting and gathering in the tropical rainforests. Sadly, most of these tribal groups have declined dramatically since coming into contact with modern people.

Cultivators

Millions more people cultivate crops within the rainforest. They mainly live off root vegetables such as cassava (manioc) but, like the hunter-gatherers, they also fish, hunt animals, and collect wild plants. They use the forest to provide extra food, medicines and a whole host of other useful products.

Cultivators will cut down patches of forest to grow their crops, and then move on when the soil is exhausted, leaving the forest to regenerate (grow back). This kind of farming is called shifting cultivation, or slash and burn agriculture. It has evolved over centuries and can be a successful way of growing food in the rainforest without destroying the environment. The key is not to cut down too large a patch at any one time and, when the patch is exhausted, to give the forest a chance to regenerate.

Slash and Burn Agriculture

Unfortunately, settlers — new arrivals from areas outside the rainforest — do not have the same skills. Unlike the traditional farmers, the settlers do not give the forest the chance to regenerate. Instead of clearing a small patch within the rainforest, the new slash and burn agriculturalists cut into the forest along a broad front.

Slash and burn agriculture is now the main cause of rainforest loss. Settlers are pushing deeper into the forests of the Amazon and South-east Asia. As they burn the forest, ash fertilizes the soil and gives the crops a short-term boost. But, within a year or two, the nutrients are washed away and the settlers have to cut down more rainforest. For many years, only rough grasses and weeds will grow on the land they have abandoned.

The Amazon Forest

About 140 tribal groups live in the rainforests of Brazil. One of these groups, the Kayapo Indians, live in the Xingu river area of the Amazon basin. These people have a detailed knowledge of the plants and animals of the rainforest, and continue to live in the same way that they have done for centuries.

Below: Campor Ashaninka Indians in Peru. These people are hunter-gatherers who are able to live in the rainforest without destroying it. Their way of life is being threatened by slash and burn farming. Researchers have calculated that on average they spend only 18 hours each week collecting the food they need.

Land Rights

Land rights are an important factor in guaranteeing a future for indigenous rainforest people. Their lives are closely connected with their land. Only with legal ownership of the lands they have traditionally inhabited can such people protect themselves from threats like illegal mining and land-grabbing.

Most nation states are of quite recent historical origin, at least compared with the length of time that forest people have occupied their lands. In spite of this, governments have rarely granted indigenous people their land rights. Governments tend to define such people as 'backward' and in need of 'civilization'. Such thinking helps governments to justify interference in their affairs.

In fact, rainforest people are quite capable of looking after themselves. All they need is the right to determine their own future.

Most Amazonian states have started to recognize the indigenous people's claim to ancestral lands, although the process is slow. The Brazilian constitution, however, does not at present recognize the right of indigenous people to own land.

Yanomami ancestral land straddles Brazil and Venezuela. National parks have been declared on both sides of the border, offering some degree of protection, if not actual ownership of the land.

Skilled Farmers

The Kayapo eat the fruits of over 250 plants, and collect hundreds of others for their nuts, tubers and leaves. They are also skilled farmers. The main crops grown in the cleared patches of forest include maize and cassava. Cassava is a root that contains a poisonous acid. The Indians pound it into pulp, and put it into long wicker tubes. The acid is squeezed out with the moisture, and the dry starch that is left behind is safe to eat.

Hunting and Fishing

The Kayapo also hunt animals, and fish in the rivers. They use bows with long arrows to shoot large animals

Left: Yanomami Indians on their way to collect food. These people are fighting a desperate battle for survival on the borderlands of Venezuela and Brazil.

such as the capybara and tapir. Blowpipes and poisoned darts are used to kill the birds and monkeys that live high up in the forest canopy. Fish are speared, shot with arrows, or caught in traps made from bundles of stems.

Occasionally a large tree is cut down to collect the honey from beehives high up in the branches. Felling the tree leaves a gap in the forest, which is used to grow medicinal plants.

Recently, the Kayapo way of life has been threatened by illegal settlers searching for gold, and the prospect of massive hydroelectric dams on the Xingu. The tribe, traditionally one of the fiercest of the Amazon, is now struggling for its survival.

The Yanomami

Another Amazonian Indian group, the Yanomami, are the largest single group in all of the Americas to have had only limited contact with the outside world. Like the Kayapo, they combine hunting and gathering with shifting cultivation. Their small gardens are a wild tangle of plants, barely distinguishable from the forest.

Having a wide variety of crops and medicinal plants helps to keep pests down. Some plants attract pests, others attract the insects that eat those pests. By using natural methods, Yanomami gardens grow very well. Eventually, the Yanomami move on to another patch and the forest takes over.

Above: A woman and her baby from the Kayapo people in Amazonia. So far, these people have managed to keep their culture relatively free from outside influence. They shave their heads and decorate their faces.

Tribes of the African Rainforest

Above: 'Epke' ceremonial costume made from raffia fibre in a rainforest village in Cameroon, West Africa. Epke is a secret society that was the forerunner of the voodoo religion.

In Africa, the Mbuti Pygmies live deep in the rainforests close to the border between Zaïre and Uganda. They hunt wild animals using bows and arrows. The varied diet of the Mbuti also includes fat beetle grubs, caterpillars, honey and many different forest plants. The Mbuti travel through the forest in search of prey. They live in simple dome-shaped huts made from bent and woven saplings, covered with leaves.

Hunters and Traders

The Mbuti are renowned hunters and skilled archers. When hunting, a group of men and their hunting dogs will spread out in a wide semicircle. They close in with cries and songs, frightening the animals towards a fixed point, where the hunters will be waiting.

The Mbuti trade with more settled groups of forest farmers to obtain things that they cannot get from the forest. The Mbuti offer forest meat, fish, honey, building materials and medicinal plants. In return the villagers provide cultivated bananas, peanuts, cassava, cooking pots, machetes and cloth. One Mbuti group called the Efe are thought to have traded with a group of shifting cultivators called the Lese for more than a thousand years. The Efe sometimes even help the Lese with gardening work like weeding and harvesting.

Social Organization

The Mbuti, like all hunter-gatherers, travel in small bands made up of just a few families. The bands travel over large distances. Their territory has to be large as game is quite scarce and should not be over-hunted. Nevertheless, the Mbuti rarely go hungry. The forest almost always provides something for them to eat.

The small hunter-gatherer bands have a relaxed social order. Everyone is more or less equal, and decisions are taken on a communal basis. If an argument develops, the group can always split up temporarily to hunt and gather in different parts of the forest.

Above and right: The hunting and gathering way of life leaves many rainforest dwellers with plenty of spare time. The pygmies of the Central African rainforest use their leisure much like people elsewhere: cooking, caring for children or just smoking a pipe.

PYGMIES

The word 'pygmy' derives from an ancient Greek word meaning 'undersized'. It is used to describe some African groups of rainforest dwellers, who are distinguished by their small size.

Since there are other rainforest peoples around the world who are small in stature, it is possible that small size represents a physical adaptation to rainforest life. A small frame makes it easier to move about in dense undergrowth and light weight helps in climbing trees. Because such an adaptation would take many thousands of years to evolve, such groups could be among the most ancient rainforest inhabitants.

Animal species that have adapted in a similar way to rainforest life are the pygmy hippopotamus and the royal antelope.

Rainforests of South-east Asia

Hunter-gatherers move around in small bands, usually of two or three families. Cultivators are able to support slightly larger communities since their farming practices help to produce more food. They usually live as groups of related families in large compounds in the rainforest.

Longhouse Communities in Sarawak
Famous among such people are the longhouse communities of Sarawak, a province of Malaysia that occupies the northern part of the island of Borneo in South-east Asia. Their buildings can accommodate up to 100 families.

The houses are raised on stilts, to protect them against a variety of hazards, such as flooding and wild animals. They are entered through ladders and trapdoors, which can be removed at night in case of attack. Until quite recently, raiding and feuding between neighbouring groups was quite common. Head-hunting (cutting off and keeping the head of a dead enemy) was a traditional activity.

The people use a hardwood called belian in the construction of their homes. The mats and baskets are made from the stems of climbing palms called rattans. Feathers, skins, antlers and tusks are used for decoration and traditional rituals. Engkabang nuts, resins and precious timbers are collected from the forest to provide a source of income for the longhouse dwellers.

Family Groups
The basic unit of the longhouse community is known as the bilek. It is made up of an elementary family group of husband, wife and children. The bilek will share one compartment in the longhouse, consisting of a living room, also called bilek, a loft (sadau), a section of the roofed gallery (ruai), and the open verandah (tanju).

The bilek-family is a self-sufficient unit. They farm their own fields and their hunting and gathering is done

Right: A Penan girl with a child on her back carries a dish of wild boar meat. Only around 650 nomadic Penan people remain in the rainforests of Sarawak. They live in temporary shelters in the forest and hunt wild pigs using blowpipes made out of palm stems.

Left: The inside of a longhouse belonging to the Kenyah Dayak tribe in Sarawak. These communal houses are built from hardwood trees. Mats and baskets are made from rattans or the stems of climbing plants.

in an area of the forest, which is owned by the longhouse as a whole. At certain busy times of the year, larger groups are formed to help with the sowing or harvesting of rice, their staple crop.

Rice Cultivation

Rice is so important to the longhouse communities that its cultivation is seen as a religious activity. Local languages have a rich and complex vocabulary dealing with rice-farming, the varieties of rice and their characteristics.

Rice is treated with great reverence. Except in the course of normal farming activities, it cannot be struck, abused or harshly treated. If it is, a ritual of apology and forgiveness must be performed. A good rice harvest ensures good fortune and happiness. A failed harvest is identified with hardship and distress.

Left: Kenyah Dayak women and children from Sarawak. The women use heavy earrings to elongate their ear lobes. These people grow crops along the river valleys. They also depend on food and other products from the rainforest. They hunt the bearded pig and collect fruits, herbs and palm-hearts from the forest. They collect precious woods, nuts and resins for sale. Feathers, skins, antlers and tusks are used for decoration and for rituals.

Uses and Abuses of the Forest

Deforestation, by whatever means, is happening at a terrifying rate. Not so long ago, rainforests occupied almost twice the area that they do now. Rainforests now cover about 8.5 million square kilometres (3.3 million square miles). According to some recent estimates, an area of tropical forest equivalent to six football pitches is being lost every minute.

A Threatened Way of Life

Almost all indigenous rainforest groups are threatened in some way or other. Often, their rights to their traditional forests lands are not recognized — or at least not enforced — by the governments of the states that they inhabit. Their land is wanted for logging, agriculture, mining or hydroelectric dams.

Without their land and forest, the lives of rainforest people have no meaning. Communities break up and individuals become labourers, often working in the very industries that have destroyed their way of life.

Traditional knowledge, built up over centuries, is lost in the space of a few years. This loss affects us all, since it is only by learning from indigenous people that we can begin to discover the true value of the rainforests.

Above: In the Amazon states of Brazil, cattle rearing is the main land use. Over 80 per cent of rainforest loss in this region has resulted from cutting and burning the natural vegetation to make pasture. Usually clearance is started by small farmers who grow crops for one or two years before the soil fertility declines. Then ranchers buy the land. Cattle grazing lasts for five to seven years before the soil is exhausted and the land left unused. The Brazilian government has until recently encouraged cattle ranching.

ROADBUILDING IN RAINFORESTS

Building roads into tropical rainforest helps to open it up for new settlers. This process is often the first stage in deforestation. Sometimes, the new roads are built by logging companies searching for valuable timber. Roads are also built by governments to gain more control over the rainforests and their inhabitants.

Satellite photographs of the Amazon rainforest show clearly how roads contribute to deforestation. These pictures show a distinctive fishbone pattern. This results from the deforestation that takes place along the main road and the many side roads that branch out from it.

Above: The BR-364 highway in Brazil runs through the Amazon states of Mato Grosso and Rondônia, on the north-west frontier of Brazil. Improvements to the BR-364 led to a huge increase in new settlers in the mid 1980s. Over two million hectares (five million acres) of forests were burnt or cleared.

The New Settlers

The settlers are often poor people from the cities, who have been encouraged by their governments to start a new life in the forest. The governments of both Brazil and Indonesia have encouraged settlers to colonize the rainforest, with disastrous consequences. In Brazil, the Polonoroeste project resettled tens of thousands of people in the rainforest as a means of reducing the population of the overcrowded south. In Indonesia, the Transmigration Programme has settled over a million people from the crowded island of Java to the rainforest in less crowded outer islands.

The new settlers do not have the same deep knowledge of the rainforest as the indigenous people. They do not know how to harvest wild resources and tend the fragile soils. Once the natural vegetation is removed, the fertility of the soil is quickly lost. After the valuable hardwoods have been cut down, there is often no way to earn money. Life can be very harsh for the new settlers.

Above: The world's largest programme of rainforest settlement has taken place in Indonesia. Some Indonesian islands like Java and Bali are amongst the most crowded places on earth. People have been encouraged to move to the country's other islands, and given rainforest land for farming. In the early 1980s, 60,000 families were moved each year. Unfortunately the land where families have settled has often been unsuitable for farming. Forests in Sumatra, for example, have been needlessly destroyed.

The Hamburger Connection

Settlers are the first stage in the process of converting the rainforest to cattle pasture. People in developed countries like to eat beef, especially hamburgers, and it takes many acres of grassland to feed a herd of cattle.

Above: A bulldozer clears the way for a road in the Andes east of Lima, capital of Peru, South America. Whether intended mainly for transport or logging, new roads help to open up the rainforest to settlers.

The Rate of Rainforest Destruction

Rainforests are being destroyed more rapidly each year. The rate of tropical rainforest loss is estimated to have increased from 11.3 million hectares (28 million acres) per year in 1980 to 19.0 million hectares (47 million acres) per year in 1990. Some countries will have no tropical rainforest left by the end of the century. Thailand, the Philippines, the Ivory Coast and Nigeria have already lost most of their rainforest. By the end of the century, only Brazil and Zaïre will have large areas of rainforest left.

Much land in the United States is given over to beef production, but not enough to meet the nation's appetite for meat. In any case, land in the United States is expensive.

Land in South America is cheaper, even when it has first to be cleared of its natural vegetation. As a result, during the last 20 years, millions of hectares of virgin rainforest in Central and South America have been cleared to make way for vast cattle ranches. Without the controls it has recently introduced, Costa Rica could expect to lose 80 per cent of its forest by the year 2000, mainly through conversion to pastureland.

The Cycle of Destruction

Usually, the land clearance is started by local people. They grow crops for a couple of years until the soil is exhausted. Commercial cattle ranchers then buy the land cheaply and turn it into pasture. This, in turn, only lasts a decade or so before the soil is exhausted.

In fact, it is difficult to make money from cattle ranching in the rainforest. In Brazil, the forest clearances were made profitable with government help. Fortunately, this has now been removed. It is hoped that the conversion of rainforest into pasture will slow down.

Plantations

Large areas of rainforest have also been cleared to make way for agricultural plantations, usually to produce crops — known as cash crops — for export overseas. Governments and commercial organizations stand to make a great deal of money if the land is used for farming on a larger scale.

If they clear the forests, and grow cash crops on large plantations, they can sell large quantities of bananas, cocoa beans, oranges and other foods to make money from the richer countries. The farmers who once used the land so caringly now work on plantations for lower wages, barely enough to feed their families. Many young people move to cities to search for work there.

Above: Hundreds of oil palm fruits grow in bunches at the end of long stalks.

Right: Workers' huts on an oil palm plantation in Cameroon, West Africa. Originally from the African rainforests, the oil palm is now grown in many tropical countries. Natural rainforests are still being cleared to plant oil palm trees.

The Story of Rubber

Rubber is the most widely planted cash crop in the tropics, and one of the most valuable. It is made from the sticky sap, or latex, of a tree which grows in the Amazon. Long before Europeans arrived in South America, the Indians knew the value of latex. The Indians called the rubber trees *cahuchu*, which means 'weeping wood'. They used the latex to make waterproof shoes and bottles, and balls to play with. It was some time before the settlers realized the value of this material, but as soon as they did — in the late 1700s — they scrambled to exploit it.

At first, only wild rubber trees were used. Indians and poor whites were pressed into service to tap the trees. Each day, they cut the bark of up to 200 trees, attached a cup to each, and went back later to collect the latex. It was exhausting work, for which they received barely enough to eat. And it left no time for them to raise their own crops.

With the invention of the automobile, more and more rubber was needed. A rubber boom took place. The forest was cut down to make way for the first plantations. Rubber seeds were taken from Brazil to Malaya and Sumatra, where similar plantations were started. The local population toiled in conditions not far from slavery to collect the rubber. Plantation owners, known as 'rubber barons', made vast fortunes. Today, most natural rubber is grown in the Far East. Very little is grown in the rubber plant's native lands.

Above: A rubber tapper collecting latex from rubber trees in a plantation in East Java, a province of Indonesia, South-east Asia. Rubber from South-east Asia led to the loss of fortunes for the rubber barons of the Amazon. The failure of Amazonian rubber was also caused by a disease called South American leaf blight. This took its toll of plantations within the region.

Right: Medicinal plants being collected in the rainforests of Amazonia. Scientists are conducting experiments to see how effective these natural remedies are. They are concerned that the habitats of these plants are being destroyed.

Timber and Logging

Wood is one of the most useful of natural materials. It is used everywhere, in construction, furniture-making and many other crafts.

The most valuable timbers come from hardwood trees. Their slow growth produces a hard, compact wood which is both strong and attractive. Softwoods, such as pines and firs, thrive in colder climates, and are faster growing. But they are not as strong as hardwoods. Some softwoods are ground into pulp for making paper.

Above: Mahogany is the most heavily traded timber of South America. Although this valuable species is widespread it is now endangered in some countries. Mahogany is used to make doors and window frames. It is also thinly sliced to make veneers to cover furniture made of cheaper wood.

Tropical Hardwood

Unfortunately, some of the best hardwoods come from tropical rainforests. These include teak, traditionally used in boat- and house-building, and mahogany, used to make furniture.

Nearly all the tropical timber that is sold around the world is logged from natural primary forests. Only a very small amount is grown in plantations. As a result, many environmentally-conscious people now avoid the use of such woods in their homes.

The Mountain Gorilla

The mountain gorilla is an endangered great ape. Only about 600 mountain gorillas remain in the wild. They live in the bamboo forest and mountain rainforest of Zaïre, Rwanda and Uganda.

Mountain gorillas were first discovered by Europeans at the beginning of this century. They have probably always been rare, but hunting and loss of their natural habitat through logging have brought mountain gorillas close to extinction. Over the years poachers have trapped baby gorillas to sell to zoos, and they have sold gorilla heads, hands and feet to collectors.

Right: Trees have been logged in the Amazon for over 300 years. Originally logging was on a small scale with valuable trees chopped down by axe. Logs were floated downstream along the major rivers. Over the past 20 years there has been an increase in logging, partly due to the building of new roads. In the search for mahogany, logging roads are spreading deeper into remote areas of forest.

Left: Child survivors squat amid logs deposited by a flash flood in the Philippines. Floods have caused the deaths of many thousands of people, as well as destroying the homes of forest dwellers. The floods have been caused by deforestation. Nearly all the timber-rich forests of the Philippines have been logged over the past 50 years.

The Philippines timber boom of the 1960s provided cheap timber and huge profits for the logging companies. Government controls on the timber industry were largely ignored. Now over 30 important timber species are threatened with extinction in the Philippines. A total logging ban will probably soon be necessary.

If properly managed, tropical rainforests could produce timber on a sustainable basis (where the trees were replaced at least at the same rate as they were cut down). Unfortunately less than one per cent of the world's tropical forests are managed in this way. In the logging process, the heavy machinery often knocks down or damages many nearby trees. Rarely is any effort made to replant new ones.

The Hardwood Trade in West Africa

The countries of West Africa have already lost most of their valuable forests. Logging began about a hundred years ago in the areas close to the coastal ports. From there, logs were shipped to European countries.

Nigeria once exported timber on a large scale, but now has to import it because there is so little left in its natural forests. Ghana has also lost about 70 per cent of its rainforest, and some of the most valuable timbers have become rare. Ghana now bans the export of logs of its slow-growing hardwood species. But the export of timber is still very important to Ghana, third only to cocoa and gold as a source of overseas income.

As the hardwoods of West Africa are being used up, timber traders from Europe are turning to the rainforests of central African countries such as Congo and Zaïre. Some of the most popular African timbers are redwoods, known as African mahoganies because they look like true mahogany from South America.

THE SEARCH FOR MINERAL WEALTH

Some rainforests are rich in minerals, as well as in plant life. Governments as well as commercial organizations are keen to extract the minerals in order to make profits, even if the cost is the destruction of an irreplaceable natural resource. The threat from mining is likely to grow as prospecting for oil and metal deposits continues in the Amazon basin and parts of Indonesia, Papua New Guinea and the Philippines.

The largest rainforest mining operation in the world is at Carajás in the Amazon. Here a huge industrial site is being built. There are iron ore mines and smelting plants, aluminium plants and dams producing hydroelectricity. The smelting plants are fuelled by charcoal produced from rainforest trees. The Grande Carajás programme will eventually transform an area of rainforest the size of Britain and France.

Plans for the mining development at Carajás included new towns in the rainforest, agriculture and cattle-ranching. So many people have moved into the area

Right: Gold mining takes place at hundreds of small sites in the Amazon. As soon as gold is found in new areas, many people arrive hoping to make their fortune. When gold was discovered in the Brazilian state of Pará, in 1967, the discovery was kept secret for ten years. Then prospectors started to move into the area. The largest single mine was the Serra Pelada mine. This gold mine attracted hundreds of thousands of miners who worked in dreadful conditions.

Left: Most of Brazil's gold miners work on their own, panning for gold in the forest. Although it is dangerous and against the law, they often use mercury to separate the gold from the ore. This causes serious pollution.

Oil Pipeline in Ecuador, South America

Oil is Ecuador's main source of foreign money. Oil was discovered in the east of the country 30 years ago. Since then, it has been extracted from 6300 sq km (2450 sq miles) of forest, and further large areas are being explored for new oil reserves. This road was built so that the pipeline could be maintained and repaired. However, it has also opened up the forest to new settlers.

Drilling and the laying of pipelines often leads to oil and chemical pollution. Wildlife reserves and National Parks have not been safe from the threat of oil exploitation.

looking for a new life that squalid slum settlements have grown up around the development. This has therefore failed to live up to the hopes of the new settlers.

The Modern Gold Rush in Amazonia

Not all mining is carried out by large commercial operations. In the Amazon, for example, the land of the Yanomami Indians was invaded about ten years ago by gold miners working as individuals. Many Indians lost their homes. Others died in fights or from diseases caught from the miners. Recently, the Brazilian government has decided to protect the Yanomami land by law. The gold mines in this area have been closed, but a great deal of unregulated mining still goes on.

Mining in Papua New Guinea

Mining is also very important in Papua New Guinea, which has some of the world's largest copper, silver and gold mines. Rich oil deposits have also been discovered. Unfortunately, the mining activities have brought major problems, including river pollution. Harmful chemicals are carried many miles downstream and have ruined fertile farmland along river flood plains.

The Future of Rainforests

Rainforests provide an enormous variety of useful products. Already, an average of one in four medicines contains substances that come from rainforest species.

This is a tiny fraction of the potential. Thousands of different fruit trees, for example, have been recorded in rainforests, although fruit from only 15 of these is sold around the world.

Unfortunately, today, rainforests are exploited in a manner that is not sustainable. Most activities destroy the forest. This is a pity, since there is no reason why the forest cannot be used as a renewable resource, keeping it almost undisturbed.

Clearly, further destruction of the rainforests must be stopped. Some rainforests can be protected in nature reserves or national parks. Equally, it must be remembered that many depend on the rainforest for their living. The best way to look after forests outside protected areas is to find uses for the forests that do not destroy them.

In this way, people can continue to live in their forest homes, animals and plants can be saved from extinction, and the forests will continue to supply the rest of us with their useful products. But even if outsiders did not benefit at all from the rainforests, they would still be important natural environments, well worth preserving in their own right.

The Amazon basin contains the world's largest remaining area of rainforest. Its very size has helped to protect it. But threats to it are growing daily, and only a small fraction has official protection.

Forest Reserves

In Brazil, one idea has been to create special areas called 'extractive reserves' in which the forests would be managed fairly and sustainably.

The first extractive reserve was created in 1989. It covers 500,000 hectares (1.25 million acres) of rainforest in the Brazilian state of Acre. Other extractive reserves have since been established in the Brazilian Amazon. By law, the forest dwellers are allowed to collect nuts, rubber and other natural products and to decide amongst themselves how to look after the forests.

The change was not easy, however, and was marked by violence. Cattle ranchers are usually only interested in cutting down rainforest. As a powerful and rich group, they let nothing stand in their way. Chico Mendes, a leader of the rubber tappers and one of the main campaigners for extractive reserves, was shot and killed in December 1988.

Managing the Forests

People need wood for many different purposes. Tropical forests have a plentiful supply and if the forests are logged carefully and allowed to regrow they can continue to provide timber for sale. In the long term, governments and timber companies would actually make more money from the forests if they were properly looked after. Once this idea is accepted, the forests are more likely to survive.

Harvesting the Brazil Nut

Brazil nuts are eaten by many Amazonian people. They are also harvested for export in Bolivia, Brazil and Peru. More than 50,000 tonnes of nuts are collected each year, all gathered by hand from trees in the rainforest. The main countries that buy brazil nuts are the United States, Britain and Germany.

The brazil nut is a perfect example of a renewable rainforest product. Brazil nut trees can only grow in wild conditions. They cannot be planted since the life cycle of the nut is dependent on so many other species. The flowers of the brazil nut tree are pollinated by a special type of bee. The male bees of the species require scent from a particular rainforest orchid in order to attract females for mating.

Without the bee species and the orchid on which it depends, brazil nut trees cannot produce nuts. Once the nuts are ripe, they have to be cracked open by large rodents called agoutis, before they can germinate.

In some parts of the Amazon the brazil nut tree is threatened by forest destruction and felling for the valuable timber of the species. Small areas of the brazil nut's forest habitat are, however, being protected within extractive reserves.

Right: A family on Komba Island near Belem, Brazil, use a dugout canoe to collect the fruit of the acai palm. This fruit is used in the manufacture of ice cream and drinks.

National Parks and Tourism

National parks and nature reserves cover only about five per cent of the tropical forest area. The creation of new protected areas is slowing down. Decisions about national parks and reserves are often made by government officials working in cities far away from the rainforests. In fact, the best people to protect the rainforests are often those who live in or near them. Nowadays, people are no longer moved out of national parks but are encouraged to help manage them.

Korup National Park, Cameroon

In Cameroon, the Korup National Park protects a very rich area of rainforest which has never been logged. Local people used to live mainly by hunting and fishing. Now they are helping to run the park. The central area of Korup is totally protected. Only a small amount of tourism is allowed. Rainforest around the centre is being used for farming. This buffer zone where people live and work adds an extra layer of protection to the undisturbed rainforest in the middle. The wild plants of the buffer zone are being studied to see if any can be used for medicines.

Madagascar

Some areas of Madagascan forest are now protected. One national park in the south of the island is home to 12 different lemur species and more than 70 different kinds of birds. New methods of farming are being tried out in the nearby forests, to take the pressure off the national park. One of the keys to conserving Madagascar's forests is to work with the local people and to ensure that they have an alternative to destroying the forest.

Sinharaja Biosphere Reserve, Sri Lanka

Most of the forests of Sri Lanka have been cleared for farming. Only small areas are now protected as reserves and national parks. The Sinharaja Biosphere Reserve protects an important area of rainforest rich in plant and bird species. Some of the plants are very useful for

Above: Korup National Park, Cameroon, has the richest rainforest left in Africa. It covers an area of 126,000 hectares (about 300,000 acres). Over 400 different kinds of tree grow there. Some of these are important timber species which are being heavily logged in other parts of the country.

Left: The Ndian River is one of the rivers which runs through the Korup National Park. These rivers are very rich in fish with over 140 different kinds found there. The local people are skilled in catching fish and shellfish. They use basket traps, nets and spring-loaded fishing poles. Fish poisons made from plants such as the poison vine and akee apple are also used. Children are very good at catching small fish in the shallower streams.

Below: Young people in Sri Lanka are encouraged to grow the rare plants they use rather than collect them from the wild. In this way the wild plants will have a chance to recover.

food, spices and medicines. Local people have collected the forest plants for centuries. Now some are becoming very rare. One species of palm, called kitul, is used to make a sweet candy called jaggery, a local treat. This palm is one of the plants which is threatened with extinction. Scientists are now studying kitul and other threatened plants of Sinharaja so that they can understand how to save them.

Tourism

Travel to exotic locations is very popular nowadays and more and more people are visiting the rainforests. Birdwatching tours take visitors into the remote forests of Africa, Asia and the Amazon. This group has travelled to Cameroon, in West Africa. Tourists bring much needed foreign income to tropical forest countries and their enthusiasm helps to raise money for forest conservation.

Saving Threatened Animal Species

Left: Two-thirds of the world's chameleon species live in Madagascar, with more than 30 species found only on the island. Chameleons are reptiles. They can change colour to match their surroundings.

Frogs are the only amphibians found in Madagascar. There are about 140 species, mostly treefrogs, living in the rainforest. New species are still being discovered.

Right: Asia's great ape, the orang utan, is another endangered species of the tropical rainforest. Orang utan means 'jungle man'. This ape spends its life in the trees, building nests of branches and twigs, and eating leaves, fruits and insects. Habitat destruction is the main threat to its survival. Fortunately some orang utans live within national parks. Sadly, orang utans are still sought after for zoos in a few countries, such as Taiwan and Japan.

Many of the world's threatened animals live in tropical rainforests. Animals great and small are under threat. The Sumatran rhinoceros, threatened by logging in Malaysia and Sumatra, is one of the most endangered animals in the world. Only about 500 of these creatures are left in the wild. Every time a tropical tree is logged many tiny insects lose their home. Some may become extinct.

Over 2500 different kinds of birds live in the tropical rainforests, which is about 30 per cent of all the bird species in the world. Now many of these are threatened as their forest habitats are destroyed. The monkey-eating eagle of Asian rainforests is now reduced to only 500 individuals. The beautifully patterned ground-rollers, birds of the Madagascan rainforests, are rapidly

Below: The magnificent jaguar is the largest wild cat in South America. Hunting and loss of forests have made this species extinct farther north in most Central American countries except for Belize.

disappearing. Unless the forests are saved, many species of parrots, toucans, hornbills and hummingbirds may be lost forever.

Ninety per cent of all monkeys, apes and their relatives live in the disappearing rainforests. Some can survive in logged forests. However, if the forests are changed into farmland and pasture, the animals are forced to retreat. Protected areas provide a safe haven for some but not all threatened animals in the rainforest. Laws are also necessary to prevent people hunting and trapping threatened species and selling them overseas.

Above: A tropical butterfly (Heliconius petiverana).

INTERNATIONAL CARE AND CONCERN

The loss of rainforests is a global problem which can only be solved if countries work together. It is not easy for different countries to agree what needs to be done. However, some international agreements have been reached to help save the rainforests and to use them wisely. Often the big problem is deciding who should pay for forest conservation.

Most of the world's tropical rainforests are found in poor countries with big international debts. Twenty years ago, banks encouraged tropical countries to borrow money to build dams and new roads. Little thought was given to how the countries would pay back the money or to make sure that the money was well spent.

The cost of repaying debts is now a big burden for African and South and Central American countries. In 1990 Brazil's foreign debt cost over three times the total value of its exports. With so much money to pay back, tropical countries often cannot afford to conserve their

The Biodiversity Convention

The Biodiversity Convention was signed at the Earth Summit in Rio de Janeiro in 1992. Each country that has joined this new agreement will develop a plan of action to protect its biodiversity. Rainforests should be helped by the agreement.

Above: People around the world signed a pledge that they would take action to help save the planet. These pledges were sent to the Earth Summit and made into the Tree of Life.

Left: In June 1992, government leaders from all over the world met in Rio de Janeiro, Brazil, to talk about the environment and to decide what new action to take to look after the Earth. This historic meeting is known as UNCED (United Nations Conference on Environment and Development) or Earth Summit. Tropical forest dwellers travelled to the Earth Summit to explain why they should be allowed to take care of their own forests. Forest conservation turned out to be a difficult subject on which to reach agreement because tropical forest countries felt they were being unfairly blamed for deforestation.

forests. Now some conservation organizations are buying part of the debts in exchange for rainforest conservation work. These are called debt-for-nature swaps.

International Agreements

Governments of countries that do not have tropical rainforests are also helping to pay for tropical forest conservation. They provide money to teach people about the rainforests, for scientists to study the forests, and for running national parks.

Countries which import tropical timber are also providing some funds to help pay for the management of tropical forests. Over 100 governments around the world are members of the International Tropical Timber Organization (ITTO). This organization has agreed a 'Target 2000' by which time all the tropical timber sold around the world will be from well-managed forests.

A few of the valuable tropical timber species have become so reduced in the wild by international trade that governments have agreed to protect them by an international agreement called CITES (Convention on International Trade in Endangered Species). Through this agreement, international trade in the Brazilian rosewood timber is banned. Exports of the African timber known as Afrormosia is only allowed with permits. CITES also bans or controls trade in a long list of other rainforest species including Asian rhinos, tigers and other big cats, parrots, monkeys and orchids.

Government officials continue to talk about new solutions for the rainforest. They realize that loss of rainforests is a global crisis and that action must be taken now to save the forests for the world in the 21st century.

Index and Glossary